Robert Morley's
second Book of
BRICKS

Robert Morley's second Book of BRICKS

Cartoons by John Minnion

Weidenfeld & Nicolson London

First published in Great Britain by
George Weidenfeld & Nicolson Ltd
91 Clapham High Street
London SW4 7TA
1981

All royalties to
the National Society for Autistic Children

ISBN 0 297 77967 2

Printed in Great Britain by
Butler & Tanner Ltd
Frome and London

Contents

BRICKS IN LITERATURE
Prof. James Sutherland 96

LIFE WITH DANNY, EMMA,
CHRISTOPHER AND JANE 141

Introduction

ROBERT MORLEY

In preparing a sequel to the first *Book of Bricks* I was, at first, somewhat hesitant. The fact that we'd sold nearly a hundred thousand copies in hardback and it is e'en now selling successfully in paperback, tempted me to believe that it might be wiser not to try to repeat our triumph. However, both George Weidenfeld and the National Society for Autistic Children convinced me we should try our luck again.

I would like to start by expressing my deep gratitude to all the contributors and especially those who, like myself, have not left the fairground and are insisting on another ride on the roller-coaster. Some, including Dame Edna Everage, Ronald Harwood and Professor James Sutherland, have very kindly researched various aspects of brick-dropping and, whatever my earlier qualms, as soon as I got round to editing this book my spirits were immeasurably lightened by the sheer fun of reading the misadventures and entering again the mad world of those who, like Theo Cowan, hailing a taxi, almost squashed to death the incumbent passenger and then dissolved into helpless laughter.

We must assume that by the time this book is published the heir apparent will have successfully wed and, while hoping the whole adventure did not prove too hazardous to the various branches of the family, it might be perhaps permissible to start with a delightful collection of Royal Bricks generously contributed by Hugo Vickers.

Mr Vickers instances a number of bricks dropped by the late Duke of Windsor. In Tasmania in his early youth and on board the Royal Train, he espied in his drawing-room an indicator revealing the speed at which he was travelling. The dial registered eleven miles an hour.

'Bloody nonsense,' he is reported to have observed. 'They might at least have seen that this was working properly.' And, adjusting what he believed to be the regulator, he inadvertently applied the vacuum-brake. The train came to an unscheduled stop and the timetable for the day was considerably disorganized, especially as His Royal Highness was loathe to take responsibility for what had occurred.

In New Zealand H.R.H. was credited with having knighted the wrong man, while in Fiji at a ball at Government House, he opened the proceedings by claiming as a partner the lady typist of the chief Indian agitator on the island. In Melbourne, when the Prime Minister pointed out his son in a far corner of the room, the Prince went happily to where two men stood and shook hands with the one in evening dress only to discover that he was a waiter. At another dinner party in Australia the guests were invited to close their eyes and draw pigs on the menu. The Prince of Wales turned to his hostess and heard himself saying, 'I shall look at you and get my inspiration.'

I have my own personal reminiscence of a brick once dropped on him by my late father-in-law. The Prince at that time was President of Buck's Club, but for some time relations between he and the President had become strained. My father-in-law was not a great reader of the gossip columns and one evening set forth blithely with the beautiful socialite Audrey Simpson for an evening on the town. At the Embassy Club, the equivalent in those days of Annabelle's, the great Luigi conducted them to a table next to one already reserved for the heir to the throne. My father-in-law was slightly nervous of his reception but when His Royal Highness arrived, all was apparently to be honey and flowers.

'My dear Buck,' said the Prince, 'how very nice to see you. I would like to introduce Mrs Simpson.'

'And may I in turn introduce *Miss* Simpson,' Buck said.

Something about the way he pronounced 'Simpson', as if it were in inverted commas, gave the unfortunate impression that they were both out with ladies of the town. My father-in-law was never spoken to again, although he narrowly escaped injury some years later on Sunningdale golf course where, as the expression has it, King Edward VIII drove through him.

Prince Edward's brother, the Duke of Gloucester, Mr Vickers reminds us, was not exactly a dab at light conversation. On one occasion, after witnessing a display of belly-dancing in Cairo, he was subsequently introduced to the performer. They sat in silence for several minutes before the Duke enquired, 'Do you know Tidworth?'

There are few instances of the present Queen ever being disconcerted or put out by the inane remarks made to her by her subjects although, when Robert Graves went to Buckingham Palace to receive a gold medal for poetry, the Queen told him it was the first time she had presented such a medal. 'Congratulations, Ma'am,' replied Graves, after which the audience terminated rather abruptly. But I prefer to think that Her Majesty had a busy day in front of her - possibly a Royal Garden Party.

It was on one of these occasions that I - flushed at the success of

my riposte to Prince Charles who had enquired what on earth I was doing there, replied, 'The same reason as yourself, sir. It's good for business,' – then found myself conducting the late Prince Chula of Siam to a chair explaining that this was an admirable vantage point to observe Her Majesty actually sipping the Earl Grey. The Prince shook me warmly by the hand, stepped over the ropes and made his way to the Royal Tea Tent where he stood for some time munching an éclair and making conversation with the Monarch.

Finally, as we step off the Royal Carpet, I am indebted to Mr Vickers for his delightful account of a dinner party presided over by Sylvia Brooke, the daughter of Lord Esher, then newly married to the last white Rajah of Sarawak. A lull in the conversation occurred, but, to her relief, she was able to announce to her guests, 'Listen, it's started to rain at last.' The guests remained dumb in silent horror as the young Ranee turned to see the old Rajah blithely relieving himself over the veranda.

Which reminds me of a tale still told at the Melbourne Club of an elderly grazier, unwilling to trust his bladder another second, seizing the sugar bowl, emptying out its contents and hastily transferring it to his lap. Alas, the sugar bowl was inadequate and for some minutes his guests were treated to the sound of rushing water. It became a favourite joke at the club for irreverent strangers to test the sugar for moisture and, on one occasion at least, demanding 'one of your dual-purpose tankards'.

I leave it to Andrew Sinclair to provide, in this volume, yet another gem of this genre. If we were giving prizes again this time, I would award it to the lady who prefers to remain anonymous but told me how, as a young girl, she was introduced to a blind man successfully manœuvring his tea-cup at a party to which she had been bidden by her mother to keep him amused. Another guest had brought her dog and our heroine, temporarily at a loss for conversation, made an extravagant play for the creature, petting him enthusiastically until the blind man enquired, 'Is that a dog you're talking to?'

'Yes,' she told him.

'Do you like dogs?' was the next question.

'Very much,' she said.

'Have you got a dog?'

'We did have a dog but he went blind and we thought it kinder to put him down.'

For me the charm of many of the stories in this book – such as Prudence Leith's account of the cat collar in the salad, or the wonderful slapstick moment when the bus conductress sat down

11

abruptly on the pavement having been yanked off her bus with her own ticket punch machine – lies in the visual images they conjure up and we have thought it best to leave most of these to your imagination.

I have sought to include in this volume not only bricks but examples of absent-mindedness, though there is not a word of truth in the remark by Billie Whitelaw that I once left my own mother-in-law on the doorstep. With Gladys Cooper, such a folly would be quite unthinkable, though in my presence I heard her retrieve a brick with brilliant fielding. Talking of a friend with whom she had had an unexpectedly boring luncheon, she told myself and Robert Hardy, who was of course also her son-in-law, that she was 'sick to death of hearing complaints about sons-in-law'. 'I told Mildred,' she explained, 'that it was simply not the slightest use hiding herself in the garden when they came round. Make the best of it, stop belly-aching, don't hope for miracles. Even if the marriage should break up, your daughter might make the same mistake or even worse next time round. I told her she must learn to live with them [here there was the slightest change of expression] and she will get as fond as I am of both of you from the very first day we met.' She was, of course, guiltless of further brick-dropping. A brick was dropped in her absence for her, though, by my father-in-law who read aloud a letter from Gladys while my wife and I sat over coffee with him: 'I am so glad Robert seems to be turning out all right after all your fore . . .'

'After all your "four" whats, Buck?' I pressed home my advantage.

He turned to my wife. 'I can never read your mother's writing,' he told her.

It was my turn again: 'I thought you were doing rather well. Might I try and decipher it?'

'I think the word is encouragement.' He stuffed the letter into his pocket and bought me another brandy. 'I don't know when I've encouraged you exactly,' he remarked a little later on regaining his composure over the Remy Martin.

'You came to the wedding,' I reminded him, 'and when the registrar took us into his holy of holies and asked if you were still alive, I was the one who volunteered to pop out and see.'

'I never thought that was very funny,' he rejoined, and we were back, mercifully, on our old footing.

Returning to the absent-minded, I recall the tale told me the other day by a lady who, regaining her car in the car park, looked with dismay at the havoc wrought by vandals: 'I realized they had neatly removed the radio cassette player. One expects that sort of thing these days, but I was amazed at the skill with which they had not only pinched the instrument panel without damaging the upholstery but also completely removed the steering wheel. It was only when I searched for the handbrake that I realized I was sitting in the back seat.'

By some curious chance I seem to have thrown away a letter from a lady who wrote me about her husband who must, therefore, remain anonymous. 'Eustace', she wrote, 'is becoming increasingly absent-minded and has lately embarked on a course of "memory-mending" by post. Anxious to test his progress the other morning, he picked up from the kitchen table my shopping list which he briefly perused then, replacing the list, he departed for the super-market, assuring me that he would return with all the items listed within the hour. When he did return, three hours later, it was to explain that although he'd undoubtedly remembered every single article on the list, when he emerged from the supermarket he was unable to remember where he'd parked the car.

' "All's well that ends well," I told him. "Let's check the groceries."

'He shook his head sadly. "I think I must have left them in the Police Station when I reported the car as stolen." '

Finally, my deep gratitude is due to you, gentle purchaser, for helping an autistic child and we hope that you will enjoy our effort on their behalf.

Katie Boyle

TELEVISION PERSONALITY AND WRITER

As a much-publicized and very genuine dog-lover, I have not one, but two stickers on my car voicing the opinion that 'Dogs Deserve Better People' and I always feel that if my own don't live well into their teens, I have failed them miserably. I have always gone in for portable dogs, and found that the old-fashioned Italian egg baskets complete with a small cushion are the best way to keep them both with me and out of everyone else's way. I'm so conscious of my dogs' comforts that I also carry a thermos-flask of water and assorted toys for them.

One day, I got into my car and had driven about a hundred yards when I saw a woman, then a man, then a child all making the most agitated gestures. (Oh well, fame is fame.) Then a woman virtually hurled herself under my wheels and, by a miracle, I managed to stop in time. When I, in turn, hurled myself out of the car to abuse her for doing something so stupid, I realized to my horror that there on the top of the car roof was Tessa (my Yorkshire terrier) sitting bolt upright in her egg basket and wondering what all the fuss was about!

Harold Evans

EDITOR OF 'THE TIMES'

I was with a party of fellow journalists and their wives at an eatery in the King's Road where they had a fiddler who came to the table to play love songs and his attentions greatly embarrassed the wife of my friend. He thought he knew the best way to cope with the unspoken entreaties. He took a £10 note from his pocket, showed it to her and then attempted to tip the man so that he would go away. To do this, without disrupting the host's conversation and upsetting him by appearing not to like the entertainment, he folded the £10 note and then leaned over the back of his chair to put it into the pocket of the violinist.

He found it difficult to get the tenner into the flap of the pocket and pushed and pushed. What he could not see, but everybody else watched with astonishment, was that he was trying to push the tenner into an opening at the top of the violinist's fly. The harder he pushed, the more the violinist bent his body to escape what he thought were amorous hands. But the violinist played gallantly on.

Brian Aldiss

SCIENCE FICTION AUTHOR

In the 1970s I was a guest at a large conference at Poznan in Poland. To give you an idea of how important it was, we were blessed by the presence of a live Russian cosmonaut – the Eastern bloc's equivalent of having the Pope to open the Birmingham Motor Show. I was the only English guest, but there were large delegations from all the eastern European states.

The official proceedings were deadly dull, but the 'après ski', as so often happens, was fun. In particular, I found myself the recipient of much hospitality from the Bulgarian group. This was before Bulgarian Technology had invented the Death Umbrella, and all was comradeship. Of course, Bulgarian national habits differ from ours: they drink fomented mares' milk, put their surname before their given names, and smoke a lot of cigarettes without incurring any Government Health Warnings. I also observed on that occasion that they have a wide variety of drinks – *kvass* apart – unknown in the West. I investigated that phenomenon whilst they plied me with questions about science fiction. In particular, they wanted to know a great deal about *Brave New World*. It so happened that I had boned up on that novel recently and was, therefore, able to respond rather fully, squeezing my replies through the language barrier, and waiting patiently, glass in hand, whilst the interpreter of the group translated what I said to the others. This took place in their suite. Rarely have I had a more attentive audience.

I told them what I saw as the sterling virtues of the novel, also pointing out a few seeming flaws. When we got to the flaws, some of them protested rather politely, somewhat in the matter of Canute, who bidst the mighty oceans deep their own appointed limits keep, without expecting much by way of response.

Finally, they had had enough and said, 'Mister Aldous, you have been very frank about your wonderful novel, and we thank you so much. You have been marvellously modest about it.'

Bill Tidy

CARTOONIST

Punch magazine, ever eager to submit their contributors to new dangers, had agreed to my idea that the life of a modern submariner warranted investigation. It wasn't my idea really but followed drinks on HMS ———— in Liverpool, where someone suggested I accompany a boat to sea and under.

Within days I was hanging, hands clasped at my side, beneath a helicopter somewhere off Gibraltar, while below me a very narrow submarine wallowed in a surprisingly brisk Mediterranean. Submarines have an aura of mystery and danger about them (What, go down in one of those things?) so I was determined to be cool and casual once I was on the thing.

Touch down. I was professionally undone, and hands pointed towards the tower or fin on which officers and ratings looked down with the detachment that the professionals delight in. The helicopter and wind noise made speech impossible, but I was a bit peeved at the sailors' wild gesticulations towards the fin. Christ, did they think I was going to walk towards the bow and jump in the sea? Smiling reassuringly I 'thumbs-upped' them and walked carefully, but knowledgeably, towards the fin. I knew from research that this type of submarine had a door in the fin. Ha, right in front of me was a nice hole for some unsuspecting idiot who had never been to sea before to

plummet down. I skirted it carefully, miming 'Yes, all
right, all right I can see it' to the wildly waving fool in the
frogman suit who was to save stupid me from falling into
it, or over the side. Do they think I am ga-ga? Confidently
I gripped the rail around the fin and inched my way along
the narrow casing to the door which was closed. No
handle! Hell, what should I do? Don't let the side down,

Tidy. I pushed the door hard. Nothing, oops, nearly slipped – bloody hell, they are all watching from the top of the tower and waving. What was that? A tap on the shoulder, and a glaring frogman pointed back to the hole in the casing. Crimson with embarrassment I retraced my path to the manhole and descended the ladder.

Below, the greeting was sincere and cheerful enough, but to a man who'd studied *Jane's Fighting Ships 1978* (£34), 'This your first time on a submarine?' was the put-down of all time.

Mrs R. Wheller

My daughter Nicola works at the Technical College in Taunton, and has been deeply involved with the organization of a comparatively new department. Recently she had occasion to show an inspection committee over the new unit.

'How do you feel, Miss Wheller,' asked one member, 'now that you've got this project off the ground?'

'Actually,' said my daughter, 'I'm exhausted after only two days into the course.'

A shocked look spread over the face of her questioner. 'I beg your pardon?' he said. 'I'm exhausted', repeated my daughter, 'and we're only two days into the course.'

'Oh, I see.' He looked relieved. 'I thought you said after two days' intercourse.'

Michael Bentine

COMEDIAN AND WRITER

I was at an audition. There was a woman singing on the stage; her voice was so awful, that I turned to the man sitting beside me and remarked upon it. He replied very frostily, 'That is my wife.' Pink with confusion, I hastily stammered, 'I didn't mean her voice was awful, only the song she was singing.' To which he replied, 'I wrote it.' I slunk away.

Diane Cilento

ACTRESS

I was returning from Australia to Italy, just after I had
produced my first child. At the time, my daughter was
about five weeks old and I was carrying her in the usual
wicker basket and was armed with mounds of nappies,
gripe water, booties and bonnets. We had already been
travelling for many hours from Sydney to Darwin, to
Singapore, and then to an unscheduled stop, Bangkok.

I was anxious to take advantage of this unexpected
stroke of luck, as I had heard that the Thai carvings,
jewellery and paintings were beautiful, cheap and unob-
tainable anywhere else.

Having left my basket-load of baby in the hands of two
enchanting ladies in the Mother's Room at the airport, I
hurried off to examine all the tempting goods displayed in
the stores. After an energetic and invigorating bout of
bargaining, I became the proud possessor of a set of
Siamese knives and forks carved with dancing figures, a
large roll of Thai silk of varying purple hues, and a poster
of some Thai boxers hurling themselves into the air at
each other.

I rushed back to the airport clutching my booty in my
arms and was hurried aboard the plane as the last flight call
had been made some time earlier. The engines roared,
sweets were passed around and I settled comfortably into
my seat, contemplating with pleasure the surprise with

which my delightful presents would be greeted. The great plane moved out on to the run-way.

As the roar of the engines gained momentum, I noticed that the chief steward and an air-hostess were whispering to each other, peering down the cabin past me, frowning and gesticulating as another hostess joined them and whispered urgently into the ear of the worried steward. It was quite clear that something was up. I wondered vaguely if we had a terrorist on board.

The sound of the great engines decreased. I glanced out of the window and in one blinding, heart-in-mouth moment the whole mystery was revealed: rushing down the run-way were two lovely old Thai ladies carrying a basket between them which they lifted up momentarily for inspection. They were shouting but I couldn't hear a word.

The body-blush stayed with me for a good twenty-four hours; the disbelief and condemnation in the eyes of my

horrified fellow passengers made the remainder of my journey quite memorable. But there is no use denying anything: I just totally and utterly forgot that I was no longer a foot-loose and fancy-free woman whose oyster was the world. Listen, it can happen to anyone. . . .

Rudolf Nureyev

BALLET DANCER

It was the last day of my holiday and I was standing on the deck of a yacht in the harbour of Piraeus outside Athens. We had just had our last bathe. There was some delay about going ashore and I suddenly decided to have one more farewell swim. I flung off my dressing gown and jumped over the side. As I hit the water I realized that I had already taken off my wet bathing trunks. It was okay while I was in the water, but a bit more difficult when I had to climb back aboard the boat. But nobody seemed to mind.

 I'm sure they weren't disappointed.

Roger McGough

POET

Last November I was invited to give a poetry reading at Walton Jail. I was pretty nervous about facing a 'captive' audience of young long-term prisoners, some of whom were in for life.

It was a filthy morning, cold, grey and rainy, and I was led into the room after much unlocking and relocking of iron doors. I took off my mac, shook it, and said cheerfully, 'Cor, it's terrible out – you're lucky to be inside.'

Tom Conti

ACTOR

This was a situation in which I didn't know how many bricks I might have dropped.

Some years ago I went to meet the producer of a series called *The Explorers*. I was then taken to meet the director. In true British fashion, I didn't listen to the name, but his face was so familiar that I knew he was an actor turned director. We chatted amicably for half an hour or so. He knew my wife's name and that I had a daughter; I complimented him on having done his homework. The film was to be made in the Australian outback and we talked of the inadvisability of taking families on the 'shoot'. I asked whether he was taking his wife with him and the ages of his children, etc., all the while struggling to think who was the owner of this so familiar face.

As I left the office the name came – along with a cold flush and a mild buzzing in the ears – Lord Snowdon. I showed nothing of course, but made my customary exit, trying to open the door the wrong way, catching my belt on the handle and trying to say a controlled 'goodbye' before calmly walking into the tea trolley in the corridor.

I tried to 'play back' the conversation. How many bricks must I have thrown at him? What ghastly questions might I have asked? What was the last thing I saw you in? Is your wife an actress?

Theatrical Bricks

RONALD HARWOOD

Theatrical bricks: the very words conjure up a flamboyant image as though to qualify for the category they have to be dropped with certain glittering panache. The truth, however, is that theatrical bricks differ very little from any other sort of brick except in two important respects: the sound they make on the way down, and the damage they do on landing. Because more often than not they are loosed by the famous or in the presence of the famous, every nuance of tone and timbre is recorded and reproduced by the wags and wits with malice and mischief. And because actors, for all their outward show of bravura, are for the most part inwardly timid, easily hurt and childlike in their need for encouragement, the theatrical brick can be a lethal missile which will dent an already insecure ego, shatter a fragile self-confidence and cause irreparable cracks in elegant and celebrated façades.

Audiences can be devastatingly, if unintentionally, savage. Perhaps because we live in the Age of Television audiences are slow to realize that stage actors can actually hear what is being said in the stalls. During a performance of *Waiting for Godot*, the well-built Peter Bull heard an elderly dowager utter in a clear voice, 'I do wish the Fat One would go!' And in Edinburgh, while watching a distinguished actress as Cleopatra, a genteel Scots landlady said to her neighbour, 'Does she not put you in the mind of Mrs Wishart?' Bricks destined to haunt.

The late Henry Kendal once told me that an elderly woman seated opposite him on a train leaned forward, tapped him on the knee and asked, 'Excuse me, but didn't you used to be Henry Kendal?' I myself was once introduced to a genial old man at a party who didn't at first catch my name and asked me to repeat it. I did so in good clear tones. Clutching my hand tightly he said, with some relief, 'Oh, thank God, I thought you said Ronald Harwood,' a moment not easily forgotten.

The printers of theatre bills also have the habit of hitting the bull's eye. In Libya I saw a poster announcing 'Edward Jackall in *The Day of the Fox*', and Athene Seyler was once billed as 'Ateeny Sailor'.

Actors are at their most vulnerable after a performance. Tired but hopeful they wait in their dressing-rooms for friends and fans to coo and congratulate. Inevitably then, the dressing-room is the most common setting for a pile-up of bricks. For example, to Robert Helpmann who had just played Hamlet, Esmé Percy is reported to have said, 'My dear, you're the best Hamlet I've seen since Sarah Bernhardt.'

Sir Seymour Hicks, famed as a light comedian, once played a loutish cruel villain who was beastly to animals and ended up by killing his father. The great Henry Irving came round to see him after the performance. 'You held the audience in the palm of your hand, my boy,' he said. Hicks was understandably flattered. 'Did I, Sir? I'm proud you think so.' 'Yes, I do,' Irving said, 'but light comedy is your game. I shouldn't annoy them with this other stuff if I were you.' There is, incidentally, an infallible method of avoiding the dressing-room brick. If you are unlucky enough to have to be back stage to see an actor after a bad performance, take a leaf out of W.S. Gilbert's book: 'My dear chap,' he used to say, '*good* isn't the word.'

The actor's natural habitat is, of course, the stage and here the damage is often self-inflicted and always public. I am told that one young man still has nightmares about the following disaster. The play was *Antony and Cleopatra*; the place Stratford-on-Avon; a full house; the long season nearing its end. Enter Antony and his servant towards the finale of the tragedy. Antony, defeated in battle, is disrobing in preparation for his suicide. 'Pluck off,' he says, wearily, in the hope that the man will remove his cloak. On that night the servant had lost all concentration, his thoughts were a million miles away. 'Pluck off,' Antony said again, a little more tersely. Still no response. *'Pluck off!'* he hissed. The servant came to and, misunderstanding, left the stage. Some say he has now left the profession.

In an amateur production of *Dracula*, the ball scene was held up by the non-appearance of the actor playing Count Alucard. The Grande Dame of the company, intending I suppose to save the situation by sheer force of wit, said in a booming Birmingham accent, 'Isn't it terrible about that man going about sucking all them people?' And Peter Wilson reports that an actress friend playing the co-conspirator in a murder mystery was startled to hear her fellow conspirator say very slowly and distinctly, 'I'll wear fingerprints so I won't leave any gloves.'

A story that nicely embraces the on-stage disaster and the insecure ego concerns a performance of *Hamlet* at the Old Vic in the late 1920s. Robert Speaight, as the Prince, lunged in the fight scene, ripped his tights and exposed himself in all his male glory to the entire house. He was a sensitive man and deeply embarrassed. The company tacitly agreed never to refer to the incident. During the course of the season Speaight also played King John and scored a great success. Ralph Michael, a member of the company, found himself beside Speaight in the gentlemen's lavatory. The two had not been particularly friendly but Michael thought he ought to pay Speaight a compliment. Standing there side by side, doing what they had to do, Ralph Michael smiled at Speaight and said, 'By the way, Bobby, may I say how much I admired your John?' Speaight glowered at him fiercely, buttoned up and fled.

One does not instantly think of directors as sensitive souls, yet one cannot help but have sympathy for Sir Peter Hall, the director of the National Theatre, when he revisited one of his productions of an opera which had been rather extravagantly re-rehearsed with a new cast by a young staff producer. Sir Peter fumed at the changes the man had made. After the performance, the two met.

Sir Peter (furious but controlled): 'Good evening.'
Staff Producer (blithely): 'Wotcher, Peter. How's tricks?'
Sir Peter (with great control): 'You've altered my production.'

Staff Producer (merrily and with a hint of suicide): 'I know. Better, isn't it?'

Another young man, fresh from university, had the nerve-racking task of directing a great actor of the old school. It could have been Sir Donald Wolfit. At the end of the first week of rehearsal the young man wanted to say something encouraging to the star who was obviously holding himself back until there was an audience out front. 'Well, Sir Donald,' the director said uncertainly, 'it's ... er ... coming along ... very nicely.' 'Coming along? My dear boy, that's *it!*'

In the theatre, one man's brick can easily become another man's witticism. What usually happens is that a brick dropped by some poor unfortunate unknown is nimbly caught by the famous and hurled back with terrible venom. Take for example the young actor who was appearing in a comedy by William Douglas-Home. After a performance one evening the young man sidled up to the play-wright and said rather grandly, 'I say, Willie, I wonder if you could give me another laugh in Act Three?' Douglas-Home's reply was masterly. 'Funny you should say that. I was about to ask you the same thing.' The inspiration of this book, Mr Robert Morley, is not unknown for his bricks but his numerous admirers, of which I am one, like to pretend that Morley-bricks are in fact Morley-witticisms. His old friend Llewellyn Rees once met Robert in Jermyn Street. The two had been firm friends in youth but had not seen each other for many years. Rees, known as Lulu, has a circlet of saintly white hair and is ideal casting for an archbishop. 'Lulu, my dear,' Robert said, 'where have you been? I haven't seen you for ages.' 'No,' replied Lulu, 'most of my friends think I'm dead.' Said Robert, 'Not if they look closely, surely?'

No discourse on theatrical bricks would be complete without reference to that Gold Medallist among brick-droppers, Sir John Gielgud. I have two favourite Gielgud-clangers. Once, when lunching at the Ivy Restaurant with the impresario Hugh 'Binkie' Beaumont and the actress Athene Seyler, Sir John discussed the casting of his next play. 'I don't know who to get for the old woman. All

36

the best actresses are busy. There's only poor old Athene left.'
Beaumont closed his eyes; Miss Seyler smiled sweetly; Sir John must
have sensed his clumsiness. 'Not you Athene,' he said quickly, 'the
other Athene.'

In 1953, Sir John took a company to Salisbury, then in Rhodesia,
now in Zimbabwe, to play *Richard II*. At the final curtain-call, he
stepped forward to make his speech. As is the custom on such
occasions, Sir John thanked all those who had made the event
possible. 'In conclusion,' he said, 'I want to thank the wonderful
stage hands. They've all worked like blacks.' They all were.

Geoffrey Bryson

A very dear friend, now alas deceased, was not noted for thinking deeply before she spoke. She was present at an entertainment in (would you believe) the Floral Hall at the Valley Gardens in Harrogate and one of the items in the show was a fairly impromptu fashion parade in which audience participation was invited. As the audience largely consisted of matronly Harrogate ladies, you can imagine what it was like. When the parade had finished, the compère - who as a professional entertainer should have known better - asked if anyone had spotted the Deliberate Mistake. My friend leapt to her feet and declared, 'Number four is a man.' Needless to say number four was a Harrogate matron in full sail.

Sally Bell

In the summer of 1966, when we were travelling on the ferry from Brindisi to Patras, I was standing patiently in a queue (very British) for coffee when Robert Morley's voice boomed over our heads – in Greek – asking for two coffees. In a flash he was served. I had to wait another ten frustrating minutes. If I'd had a brick I would have dropped it in his coffee!

 ΔΕΝ ΦΤΕΩ ΕΓΩ ΑΝ ΔΕΝ ΜΙΛΑΣ ΤΗΝ ΓΛΩΣ-
ΣΑΝ ΚΥΡΙΑ. ΕΣ ΑΛΛΟΥ ΕΚΕΙΝΕΣ ΤΙΣ ΜΕΡΕΣ
ΣΥΧΝΑ ΜΕ ΣΥΝΧΗΖΑΝ ΜΕ ΤΟΝ ΜΑΚΑΡ-
ΙΤΗΝ ΚΥΡΙΟΝ ΟΝΑΣΗ.

Carol Channing

COMEDIENNE

I was living in a rather smart apartment block in New York some years ago when, one morning, I discovered that my telephone was out of order. I had a very busy day ahead and a lot of calls to make, so I rushed downstairs to speak to our switchboard operator who handled all the calls for the building. Whilst I waited impatiently to speak to her, I distinctly heard her say, 'Oh yes, ma'am, I'll gladly book that call for you if you'll just confirm your full name – is it *Mrs* or *Miss* Duchess of Windsor?'

Tony Benn

MEMBER OF PARLIAMENT

This true story concerns the late Percy Wells, who was the MP for Faversham in Kent. His last train from Victoria Station ran at about 10.30 p.m. and therefore he was always anxious that he might miss it when we had a division at the end of the Commons debate at 10.00 p.m.

As a result, he used to push himself to the front of Members queueing up in the Division Lobby and, as soon as the doors opened, he would rush through and, having been counted in the Division, would dash downstairs and get a bus to Victoria Station to catch his train.

We all knew this and so we used to make way for Percy to push to the head of the queue night after night.

One night Percy brought his wife to dinner at the House and after dinner they were sitting having a cup of coffee when the Division Bell rang for the ten o'clock vote. Percy went upstairs into the Division Lobby, where colleagues pushed him to the front as usual, and then he rushed off to Victoria Station, where he caught the last train. But, when he got home, the lights were out and the house was locked, and he realized that he had left his wife sitting in the House of Commons. She presumably discovered what had happened after an hour or two and was obliged to spend the night in a hotel in London.

This story went round the House of Commons very quickly and ever after that, whenever there was a late vote, people used to make way for Percy and push him to the front, but they would always tap him on the shoulder and say, 'Have you got your wife with you, Percy?'

Percy was a charming, modest man, and this story used to amuse and embarrass him at one and the same time.

George Moor

For years I had taken the old pony through the woods to the stable. The path was very crumbly and dangerous at one point and I was using my accustomed soothing phrases when I noticed that I was addressing my bicycle.

Lord Clark

ART HISTORIAN AND AUTHOR

Although I have been elected to nine clubs and have paid the entrance fees, I have resigned from all but one simply because I have been too embarrassed to speak to any of the members. This is a ridiculous shortcoming, the more so as I am very fond of talking; but I am still unable to conquer it. My only recent effort to be clubable confirmed my fears. A dinner was given in the St James's Club for Oliver Chandos, who had been its chairman for many years and had just been made a Knight of the Garter. As he was an old friend of mine, I thought I ought to attend. I found myself among a group of members, none of whom I remembered having seen, who naturally did not address a word to me. After about ten minutes a man who looked like a Naval Officer, wearing a claret-coloured bow-tie, advanced towards me and said, 'You're Sir Kenneth Clark.'

I agreed.

'The Bart, of course,' he said.

'No,' I said, 'I am not a baronet.'

'But you must be,' he said, 'the other Sir Kenneth Clark is a fearful shit; everybody says so.'

'Well, I'm afraid I'm the only one.'

Simon Curtis

STUDENT

Early last year, soon after starting at a college in North Carolina, I was introduced to two attractive girls in the campus bar. One was coloured and the other white. I invited them to have a drink and they both asked for wine.

'Well, what's it to be,' I eagerly enquired, 'white or black?'

Leonard P. Belson

OPTICIAN

Every optician spends a considerable amount of his professional life adjusting spectacles which, through normal wear, have become loose or uncomfortable. We become quite used to hearing tales of woe from our patients who have sat on their spectacles, lost their screws or are suffering from broken 'arms' and 'legs'. But the demure, little old lady who confronted me this time was completely original.

'Can you tighten me specs, luv?' she asked. 'They drops orf every time I goes to the toilet'.

My waiting-room, crowded with patients, suddenly came alive. Magazines with the latest news of the *Titanic* and eye-witness reports of the crash of the R.101 were put down and all heads swivelled round at this unheard-of phenomenon. I knew instinctively that I should not ask the inevitable question, but curiosity got the better of me.

'How can your spectacles fall off when you go to the toilet?' I asked.

I was treated to the type of withering look reserved for the imbecile, as she bent down to illustrate her reply: 'Simple, luv. When I bends dahn to pick up me knickers, they falls orf!'

 Good enough for *Punch*, in which periodical circa 1900 I feel it must have been illustrated by the late George Belcher.

Lady Diana Cooper

AUTHOR

Not recognizing people has always been the cause of dropping bricks. I'm always telling people grotesque stories – which turn out to be about themselves.

The other day, when thousands of us were celebrating Sir Robert Mayer's hundredth birthday at the Royal Festival Hall, five hundred of us repaired to a special room during the *entr'acte*. There I was mooching around without an escort, when a nice little woman equally unescorted came to my side to ask me if I did not think it wonderful.

'Wonderful,' I replied, 'and isn't he marvellous?'

'Marvellous,' she replied, and so we rippled on in praise off-handedly for several minutes – during which time I noticed the size, sparkle and splendour of the diamonds round her throat.

The penny dropped. I bungled an arthritic 'bob' saying, 'Oh, Ma'am. Please, Ma'am. I'm so sorry, Ma'am – I didn't recognize you without your crown.'

Neither surprised nor coldly, she said, 'I thought it was Sir Robert's night, not mine.'

Of course I've dropped much more hurtful bricks all my life – through my eyes, not my heart.

Terry-Thomas

ACTOR AND COMEDIAN

I was fifteen and on summer holidays in Coombe Martin, and very ambitiously invited two girls and their very severe mother to tea in a grotto café in Lynmouth.

Having rehearsed the ordering of the tea, I was able to converse with the waitress in a lordly manner. I then relaxed for a few seconds, beaming with satisfaction at my impressed guests. Suddenly something clicked and I realized I had forgotten a vital ingredient. 'Waitress,' I called, 'I nearly forgot to order my very favourites – please add some Lemon Turd Carts.'

John Cleese

ACTOR AND WRITER

My favourite absent-minded story concerns (I believe) Soren Kierkegaard, the Danish philosopher. He wandered off one morning deep in thought and entered his local park. Utterly distracted by the demands of the problem that was absorbing him at that moment, he wandered across the lawns and right into the middle of a huge flower bed.

He was brought back to consciousness by an irate head gardener rushing towards him shouting, 'What are you *doing* there?'

'What are *any* of us doing here?' cried Kierkegaard.

Cynthia Isserlis

My mother to my husband: 'Oh, George, you *must* come and live in Suffolk. It's such a wonderful place for widows!'

Paul Dew

I once visited the home of a friend to leave a message concerning a jumble sale which we were jointly organizing. When I looked in the front door along his passage I saw a number of boxes containing clothes.

'Collecting plenty of stuff for the jumble sale I see,' I remarked to him, 'but I'm afraid you'll have a bit of a job with some of this by the look of it.'

'I happen,' he told me, 'to be rebuilding my wardrobe upstairs.'

Norman P. Coxall

In the 1960s, when London was swinging, the Beatles were at their peak and Carnaby Street was the Mecca of all the young trendies, it was very smart amongst the young set to go to 'in' places such as bistros or bistro-theques (which is a bistro and discotheque combined). The society photographer Tom Hustler ran such a place in Maddox Street called Fanny's; it's probably still in existence today.

My friend and I booked a table and took along two girls we hoped to impress. We told the girls that we were involved in Music and Fashion and anything else we considered to be remotely trendy, and they were very impressed.

On reaching the bistro, we were shown to our table and the waiter busied himself with the menus and napkins.

'Is young Hustler in tonight?' my friend enquired.

'You mean Tom Hustler, the guy that owns this place?' said the waiter.

'Yes, of course I do,' replied my friend. 'We're great chums.' This really impressed the girls.

'That's odd,' said the waiter, 'I'm Tom Hustler and I've never seen you before in my life.'

Lady Antonia Fraser

BIOGRAPHER AND MYSTERY WRITER

I have a particular fondness for literary bricks, having started very promisingly in my teens by insisting on conducting a whole conversation on the assumption that a man called Tristram Shandy wrote a book called *Laurence Sterne*. In vain my interlocutor tried, tactfully, to put me right. I gamely battled on: 'Ah, but Shandy's understanding of Sterne ...' It might sound rather brilliant these days.

Two other literary bricks concern my great-uncle and aunt, Eddie and Beatrice Dunsany. Aunt Beatrice charmed me as a child with the story of the rich and romantic American Lady touring Europe – before the First World War, I imagine. She was enchanted with the Europeans – especially the titled ones. Overhearing a conversation about Machiavelli's *The Prince*, she contributed enthusiastically: 'Oh, the dear Prince! We met last fall and I just fell in love with him. . . .'

Uncle Eddie Dunsany – a man of wonderful and terrifying aspect – casually referred to a book called *Peace and War* during a conversation about Tolstoy with Maurice Bowra (then a young don). For a while Maurice Bowra managed to keep the conversation going without mentioning the title at all, thus avoiding the twin perils of contradicting his host and compromising himself. Finally, trapped by the turn the talk had taken and deciding to go

for politeness, he too alluded to *Peace and War*.

'*Peace and War! Peace and War!*' roared Uncle Eddie.
'You mean *War and Peace.*' And he retired absolutely
delighted with the low level of culture among young
Oxford dons.

Irene Handl

ACTRESS

Shambolic night began like any other night of my season at Watford. We were doing *Blithe Spirit*, a play which I adore, and I was playing a part which I adore, Madame Arcati. The company was in great nick, the laughs had been coming a treat right through the show. Only the last act to go: I arrive at Charles Constandine's house at the witching hour, fetchingly clad in Chinese pyjamas, bowed down by assorted herbs and strings of garlic, plus a deep sense of shame at my failure to definitively de-materialize that teasing, obdurate sprite Elvira.

I put my herbs down somewhere handy, in case they are needed for last-ditch tactics, and am starting on preliminary incantations when I become aware of a sensation that cannot be but recognized throughout the civilized world: the unmistakeable slither of trousers falling down. Suavely, inexorably my black satin trousers slid down towards my ankles, where they were firmly taken into custody by Madame Arcati's cycle clips. I was left standing in my Chinese jacket, my suspendered hose and my private underwear – a single garment of silk and lace known to the lingerie trade as 'cami-knickers'. Mine were red – a beautiful cerise, which lights more brilliantly than anything I know except tinned cherries.

The actor playing Charles's part exploded. Gripped by the terrible clips, I shambled into what I hoped would be the dimmest corner of the stage and tried to effect repairs. No use: the divorced ends of the waistbelt refused to be re-united and I would have to play the rest of the scene holding everything up. Ostrich-like I had my back to the house, so I didn't know that a malign moonbeam was lighting my tinned cherries.

After that nothing seemed to matter, as the whole place went up in an explosion of laughter which could be heard out in the street and wasn't extinguished on either side of the curtain till long after it had finally come down.

Olwyn Holden

One Easter Sunday morning my husband sneaked a caramel chocolate from our daughter's Easter egg. The next moment he was writhing in agony, the chocolate having impacted or trapped a nerve in a tooth. I rang the dentist, who offered to come down to his surgery in about one hour's time. I then rang the doctor who said to come over to his house and collect two very powerful painkillers. I jumped in my car and drove the twenty minutes to his house, twenty minutes back, to find my husband practically passing out with pain. I rushed into the kitchen, poured a glass of water, and swallowed the tablets myself.

Hunter Davies

AUTHOR AND JOURNALIST

When my wife, Margaret Forster, went up to Oxford in 1969, fresh from her council estate in Carlisle, all the other girls in her college, Sommerville, seemed to be the daughters of famous people. There was Teresa Waugh who turned out to be the daughter of Evelyn, Julia Gaitskell, the daughter of Hugh, Judith Pakenham, a genuine Pakenham, and Annabel Asquith – a real Asquith.

In an effort to keep up her end, she started agreeing that the novelist E.M. Forster was her father. In those days, Mr Forster's private life had not been extravagantly explored and no one, apparently, expressed disbelief. Years later, however, an academic from an American University somehow heard the legend and wrote to my wife for confirmation. Had E.M. Forster been secretly married and would she supply some information about her mother?

By this time Mr Forster was, of course, dead and his version of the love that dare not speak its name had been published posthumously.

Lord Delfont

IMPRESARIO

Joe, feeling unwell, went to his doctor for a check-up. After a thorough examination the doctor pronounced that Joe only had a short time to live.

Shocked, the doomed man said, 'Will the end come in months or years?'

'No,' said the doctor, 'in a matter of hours, and, if I were you, I'd go home to bed and make myself comfortable.'

Joe did this but, becoming nervous, he called his friend Mo and said, 'I'm dying. Won't you come over and talk with me in my last hours?'

Mo did as he was asked and, after some hours of reminiscing, he fell asleep. Joe immediately roused him and said, 'Please, Mo, don't go to sleep now.'

Mo rubbed his eyes and grumbled, 'It's all right for you, but I've got to go to work in the morning.'

Serena Fass

TRAVEL AGENT

A friend of mine was driving along happily minding his own business, when all of a sudden a woman driver came tearing round the corner in the opposite direction on the wrong side of the road. Passing him, she rolled down the window and shouted 'Pig'. My friend, quite astonished by this insult, went on his way, muttering 'Silly old cow'. On turning the corner he drove straight into a herd of pigs.

Sir Fitzroy Maclean

AUTHOR

Some thirty odd years ago, as a very young and rather nervous Member of Parliament, I stayed a week-end with a prominent and influential constituent. His wife, also a pillar of the local establishment, had a fine head of red hair.

I have always been fascinated by the contents of other people's medicine cupboards. Combined with a strong urge to experiment, I have also always held the possibly rather dangerous view that, whatever it does to other people, no medicament is likely to have any effect on me. That night in the medicine cupboard I found a large bottle labelled 'peroxide'. I had heard of 'peroxide blondes', then much in vogue. My hair in those days was dark brown. 'I bet,' I said to myself, 'this stuff doesn't make *me* go blond,' and, rubbing several lavish handfuls into my hair, I went to bed.

When I woke up next morning and looked in the looking-glass, I found to my amazement that my hair had in fact turned bright red, exactly the same colour as that of my hostess, who, as she presided over the breakfast table, quite clearly viewed me with the wildest surmise. Since then I have been rather more careful – at any rate with peroxide.

Cleo Laine

SINGER

Like lots of mothers with first-borns and first walks to the shops, I left my baby outside the butcher's and walked back home alone. While preparing the tea, I experienced a strong feeling of loss, of something misplaced. When my mother came in to ask where young Stuart was, I didn't wait to reply but sprinted back to find him quite happy, still outside the family butcher's shop.

Our third child also suffered, but not in the same way. Moving to a new house necessitated a change of school for young Jacqueline, my daughter. I enrolled her at the village school and proudly took her on the first day. Arriving home after school, we questioned her about what she'd done. She wasn't very forthcoming, but pressed further said, 'Well, it's a bit babyish for me.' A little worried, we went to see the Headmistress.

Talking through the problem, she took our Jackie's enrolment papers and said, 'Let's see, she was born in 1964, so she *should* be in the infants, but as she seems so advanced we will ...'

'What year did you say?' asked her father.

'1964,' repeated the Headmistress.

John looked at me knowingly and accusingly: 'You made Jackie a year too young, she was born in 1963.'

The Headmistress quietly closed the folder: 'I think someone should come back and have arithmetic lessons, don't you?'

Sir Nicholas Henderson

AMBASSADOR

Before paying an official visit to a town in France, I was given the usual briefing about leading personalities so as to help make the *entente* as *cordiale* as possible. I was told that the Préfet's wife was pregnant and that the Mayor's wife was very ill. At my first meeting I expressed pleasure and congratulations over the happy family news I had heard; at my second I commiserated, saying that I hoped Madame's condition would soon be *rétablie*, a phrase I had mastered with pride.

It was only after both interlocutors had remarked upon the eccentricities of the British and the pleasure that they had had in experiencing it at first hand that I made enquiries and discovered that I had got them the wrong way round.

John Gardner

JOURNALIST

After the war, I was – like most hopeless sons – destined for the Church, as my father was a High Anglican priest. I took my degree at Cambridge and then went on to complete things at a theological college in Oxford (saw the light there, also, and became a journalist instead).

The theological college was, naturally, very high church and strict. During one Holy Week, I found myself in a whirl of services and much ritual. Easter came

and, having given up the cinema during Lent, I took myself off to the pictures at the earliest, and most seemly, opportunity.

The rigours of religious ritual must have really got to me. As the performance ended, I left my seat, gravely genuflected to the screen, and only realized what I had done when I saw people looking at me. I left with red cheeks. The film was, in fact, one of the early *Carry On* movies.

Margaret Drabble

NOVELIST AND BIOGRAPHER

How I welcome this opportunity to relive one of the nastiest moments of my life! It occurred when I was watching for the first time what I think is called a rough cut of the only film I ever wrote that ever got made. Naturally I found my own story deeply moving, and was weeping copiously by the end. However I was not so far carried away as to forget that I was sitting next to the composer of the music, to whom I had just been introduced. Politely I blew my nose, turned to him, and said, 'I thought the music was wonderful.' He looked surprised (or was it offended, I dare not recall) and said, 'But I haven't written it yet.' I think I went on to explain that I wasn't really very musical, that I was in fact tone deaf, but I don't suppose it did much good.

Norman Plastow

ARCHITECT

I worked for several years with a Hungarian woman architect whose command of the English language made one realize how versatile and subtle it can be. One of her best efforts occurred at a meeting where a scheme for an old people's home was being discussed. The discussion was brought to an abrupt halt by her profound observation: 'A woman is as old as a man feels her, but a man is as old as he feels himself.'

Lord Longford

AUTHOR AND CAMPAIGNER

I recently attended a film show given by my old friend
Aidan Crawley, the famous cricketer, etc., following his
travels in the Himalayas. On the way in I saw a rather
lonely figure sitting in the corridor. It was the great ex-
plorer Sir John (now Lord) Hunt. I said to him cordially,
if a trifle condescendingly: 'You look a bit lonely, John.
Why don't you come in with our party?' Lord Hunt is the
most modest man in the world. It is said that when he
received an invitation to become a Knight of the Garter he
thought it must have been intended for the other Lord
Hunt. After considerable hesitation, he explained to me:
'They've made me the President here [that is of the Royal
Geographical Society]. I'm afraid they want me to take
the Chair.'

James Herriot

VET AND AUTHOR

My absentmindedness, though constant and long-standing, has usually manifested itself in trivial ways. Brushing my teeth with shaving cream and wondering why the new toothpaste tasted so foul and made me foam at the mouth. Stopping in the middle of a veterinary round and trying to think where the devil I was going. Forgetting to put my dog back into the car after a country walk and having to dash back to the spot where, showing more sense than his master, he would be patiently waiting. Enclosing letters in the wrong envelopes with wildly embarrassing results.

However, there are two incidents which, though not world-shaking, may have caused certain people to doubt my sanity.

The first was when my wife asked me to take the sitting-room clock to be repaired. With my two young children in the car I drove into the market place of our little town and, clock under arm, entered the shop. Only it wasn't the right shop, it was the butcher's. My children, who always delighted in their father's affliction, watched, giggling, as, with my thoughts far away, I stood staring into the butcher's eyes.

I had been a customer for a long time and the good man smiled in anticipation as he twirled his cleaver in his hand and I clutched my clock. This went on for several very long seconds before I realized where I was. There is no doubt I should have calmly purchased a pound of sausages, but my return to the world was too sudden, the prospect of explanation too unthinkable. I merely nodded briefly and left.

The other man in our town who probably thinks I am unhinged is a Mr Craythorne. Some years ago he was manager of Mead's grocer's shop, his children went to the same school as mine and he and I knew each other quite intimately.

He was standing in the doorway of his shop one day when I passed, my brain, as usual, wrestling with some distant problem, my eyes staring into space.

I heard his voice: 'Now then, Mr Herriot,' and turned a blank gaze on him.

Only fellow sufferers will understand that at that moment I had not the remotest idea who he was. To whom, I desperately cogitated, belonged this very familiar face? Then, as I floundered, I noticed the word 'MEAD' in foot-high letters above the shop window.

'Good morning, Mead,' I cried heartily, giving him a smile compounded of friendliness and relief.

I had gone only a few steps before I realized that my greeting had been not only impolite but somewhat arrogant. I turned back and addressed him again.

'Good morning, *Mister* Mead,' I said.

It was only when I had turned the corner of the street and come to the surface that it dawned on me, too late, that his name was Craythorne and the time was late afternoon.

Andrew Sinclair

NOVELIST AND BIOGRAPHER

A friend of mine from Australia was asked to an elegant party in Eaton Square. Caviar was to be served after the champagne. Having drunk too much of that, my friend found his way to the bathroom. He groped around for a light switch, but did not discover it. He then groped around for a lavatory, but did not discover one. Finally, he found the edge of the bath and settled for that. He relieved himself slowly and fully, then turned on the taps to swill away the evidence.

Going back to the party, he asked his hostess where the caviar might be. 'Packed on ice,' she said, 'in the bath. I am just going to get it.' He went instead, walking quickly back to Australia.

Dame Edna's Bricks

Many moons ago, long before I became a bi-hemispheric megastar, my manager Barry Humphries was at a function in Oxford. Who should he bump into there but Sir Osbert Lancaster, the clever cartoonist, who was then just plain Mister Lancaster. Barry introduced himself as an Australian comedian, but he must have mumbled his name with uncharacteristic modesty because Sir Osbert said: 'The only other Australian comedian I know is that awful chap who dresses up as a housewife and waves daffodils.' I bet Barry went a bit quiet after that.

Mind you, possums, it's funny the number of people who used to think Barry was one of those twisted types who went in for female impersonation. Just because he and I are never photographed together is no reason to believe that Mr Humphries sometimes dresses up as me! What a sick suggestion that is.

However, a few years ago, when I went to Royal Ascot, an incident occurred which reminded me how many intelligent people still believe this libellous rumour.

At the race meeting in question I wore a gorgeous hat based on the Sydney Opera House, Casino and multi-purpose conference and convention complex. It was so spectacular that it attracted the world media and, I'm afraid, rather 'up-staged' a very famous lady whose Ascot hats usually make headlines year after year. As luck would have it, she and I bumped into each other outside the gates, and as the cameras jostled to snap us for posterity, her son (who also designs her clever hats) said to me rather sharpish: 'At least my mother is a *real* woman!'

Would you call that a brick possums?

Talking of incredible mothers, it was my own wonderful mother who once said to me: 'Edna, every time you open your mouth it's just to change feet.'

The day came when I had to bundle her off to the St Peter's Close Twilight Home in Melbourne, and she naturally - bless her! - wanted to pack her entire lifetime's collection of memorabilia.

'You'll only need a nightie and a toothbrush, darling,' I said gently as the attendants escorted her caringly into their spotless unmarked van. 'If you happen to need any of your favourite old frocks or bygones, tell matron and we can always fetch them out of the incinerator.'

What a ghastly slip of the tongue that was because I'd meant to say wardrobe. Luckily, my precious old parent had her mind else-where at the time - as she so often had in those days - so my 'brick' fell on deaf ears, but Mummy certainly wouldn't have thanked me if she'd known what a big spring-cleaning we had planned just as soon as she had been comfortably re-allocated. I know Oxfam wouldn't have been overjoyed to receive my precious darling's mammoth collection of nostalgia and moth-fodder.

I'm glad super old showbiz chum Robert Morley has asked me to rack my brains to recall any little bricks I've dropped, because quite frankly there have been times in my career when something un-toward has popped out that shouldn't have. Most married women have had the same experience!

There was the time when a famous female member of the Royal Family (no names, no pack-drill) once visited me in some distress at the Dorchester Hotel in Park Lane Street and flung herself sobbing into my arms. The first thing I said was, 'How did you get past my security, darling?' Again I was saved from embarrassment because the poor little mite was, for once, too upset to have noticed my big macho bodyguard discreetly stationed outside the door.

On another occasion I was at a Royal Garden Party in the gardens of the Queen's gorgeous period home at the end of Mall Street and to my embarrassment an enormous queue of distin-guished guests and upper-echelon high-fliers thought they recog-nized me and besieged me for autographs. Normally I would have obliged with pleasure, but that day I felt I owed my sovereign a word of apology for slightly up-staging her (to use a show business term). 'Oh, Ma'am,' I blurted out, 'if I'd known that this was going to happen, I'd never have worn my tiara.' My hostess smiled charmingly but not without a funny little hint that I'd put my Gucci peep-toe sling-back in it well and truly.

Christina Foyle

BOOKSELLER

In the 1930s, I spent a holiday in America and watched Duke Ellington perform to an enraptured audience.

Coming home on the ship, we met some rich Americans, who were very conscious of their wealth and importance. One of them said to me, 'My, I am looking forward to seeing your country. Do you know, I am related to Duke Ellington?'

'Really?' I said. 'We saw him perform with his band in New York and he was wonderful.'

'I said the Duke of Wellington,' was the frosty reply.

Yehudi Menuhin

MUSICIAN

My wife agonizes between my infinite capacity for forgetting names and my equal skill in triumphantly misap-
propriating them. Of the two habits, she would appear to
prefer the former, for at least, she says desperately, she can
be called upon like some dematerialized telephone direc-
tory to furnish me with the missing name. Whereas with
the latter she has, as it were, hastily to erase the misnomer
with as much speed and tact as possible, redressing the
balance with a sweet smile for the victim and a venomous
glance at myself.

The illustrations I could offer of this kind are so
numerous that it is difficult to choose from among them.
However, one particular instance I remember taking place
in the foyer of the little Opera House in Monte Carlo. It
must have been, I suppose, after one of my concerts,
which in that sociable spot are never left unadorned by
some party to send the muscian happily off to bed however poorly he may have played.

There was a milling crowd of overdressed people of
both sexes – by which I don't mean over-covered but
rather under-draped – the women with large expanses of
flesh leaving a splendid field for jewellery and men in
dinner-jackets made of every imaginable material from
plum-coloured plush to Turkey carpet (circa 1910).

Diana, with our youngest son Jeremy in tow, had become separated from me – a most dangerous situation socially – and I suddenly espied a smallish man with a shock of white hair, a brown face and alert black eyes. Darting forwards, for fear he would be engulfed before I could nab him, I seized him by the shoulders, embraced him on either cheek, exclaiming delightedly: 'Chagall! *Cher Marc, comment ça va?*'

The expression of blank surprise on the face of the assaulted man totally failed to deflect my joy and I continued in much the same vein, asking him what new work he was doing (oils or water-colour?) and it wasn't until my hands – possibly more perceptive than my eyes or mind – registering the thick furry white flannel of his jacket (the poor fellow was still imprisoned in my grip) that I sensed dimly that something was awry.

Releasing my captive uneasily, I turned to find Diana at my elbow and muttered to her 'Chagall, darling,' in a kind of dying fall. She, of course, had taken in the utter stranger at one glance – ghastly 'who's for tennis' jacket, black satin propellor of a black tie, velvet shoes and all – and placed him somewhere half-way down the list of Greek ship-owners without whose drachmas the tower-blocks and gambling temples of that once exquisite little town would have tumbled into the sea. Offering an apology with her second-best smile, she extricated me from my predicament, adding that, especially after a concert, my faculties were dimmer than usual and that, in order to protect herself, she usually greeted me back-stage with a kiss and the reminder that she was my second wife – a position that she had by then stoutly maintained for some thirty years or so.

With true Greek courtesy, the utter stranger told me that he considered I had bestowed upon him a great compliment and that he was indeed often mistaken for Chagall. I turned triumphantly towards Diana and was discomfited by a veiled glare tinged with desperation. 'Well,' she said, 'at least you didn't mistake him for Indira Gandhi.'

Jeremy Thorpe

FORMER LEADER OF
THE LIBERAL PARTY

Princess Beatrice, who was one of Queen Victoria's daughters, was sitting next to a rather pompous, ill-informed politician, who in order to make conversation said, 'Ma'am, I've just come back from Spain. Is it a country you know?' To which the Princess replied, 'Oh, yes indeed. My daughter is Queen there you know.'

Frankie Howerd

COMEDIAN

Just before the last General Election, I was attending a
Sunday luncheon party. I entered the room looking for a
friendly face, when a man came forward and held out his
hand. I thought to myself, 'Good, somebody I recognize –
Peter Saunders, the impresario who presented *The Mouse-
trap*.' So I said cheerily, 'Hello, are you still running? Is
business good?' And he replied, 'I'll let you know soon.'
'Funny,' I thought, 'what a strange reply.' It took me
thirty seconds to realize that it was in fact Lord Carring-
ton, who the following week became Foreign Secretary.

Hilary Fletcher

I was travelling to a friend's home and wasn't sure where to get off the bus; when I did decide, I left it until a large queue was half-way through getting on. I darted through them in a panic and in my hurry I got my handbag strap caught around the bus conductress's ticket machine and yanked her off with me. As she sat on the kerb, the entire bus collapsed with laughter, including me, and I had to make a quick exit because for some strange reason she didn't seem to find it funny.

Billie Whitelaw

ACTRESS

Life for those who know me can be perilous, because
I'm sometimes very absent-minded. I've never left my
mother-in-law behind on the doorstep (as Robert Morley
has apparently done), but I did once lock my mother into
the lavatory for a couple of hours before I noticed she was
missing. But the most excrutiatingly absent-minded thing
I've ever done occurred at a lunch given by the Variety
Club of Great Britain. At the lunch was a very well-
known actor who had been married to a very well-known
actress. He and I talked for a while, and he told me how ill
and unhappy he had been since their divorce. I decided he
needed cheering up, so I said in my brightest voice, 'Oh,
good. There's a very dear friend of mine across the room.
I know you'll like her – you must come and meet her.'

It wasn't until my two friends stood staring in horror at
each other that I realized I'd introduced the actor to his ex-
wife. I wanted to die and I still have nightmares about it.

Frank Muir

WRITER AND BROADCASTER

I once dropped an awesome brick in circumstances so weird that the whole thing, like so many true happenings, comes out like a lie so implausible as to be an insult to the reader's intelligence.

I once ran over a man when my car was standing stock still at traffic lights. It was many years ago and the traffic lights were at the top of that little hill in Camden Town. It was a Sunday morning and I was driving to a lunch party with friends who lived in Ongar. I had no idea how to get to Ongar but, as I was setting off, somebody told me to follow the red Singer sports car of a friend who was also going to the party. The trouble was that the friend did not know that I was following him, so I had to keep his car in sight. All went well until the beastly lights in Camden Town went red just after he had crossed, trapping me. I sat fuming at the wheel, watching the red car getting smaller and smaller in the distance. Just as the lights changed to green and I was reaching for the handbrake I saw out of the corner of my eye a man backing out of the paper shop across the pavement. He was making amiable remarks to somebody inside the shop. Waving happily to his invisible friend he backed towards me, stumbled, fell over the kerb, rolled over and wedged himself firmly under my front nearside wheel.

The little red car had disappeared from view round

some corner which I would never find, and my chances of getting a free hot meal went with it. In a sudden rage I wound the window down and shouted at the flustered face two feet away: 'You ... You ... You c ...!

It was then that I noticed his clerical collar.

Gaia Servadio

AUTHOR AND JOURNALIST

I had been promised one of those things which make journalists happy and which could rightfully be regarded as a sign of acute masochism by those outside the trade: to be granted a special visa for a visit to the car factory at Togliattigrad on the Volga. In fact, I must say right away that the visa never materialized since the Soviet factory, which had been provided by FIAT, was running into disastrous delays and was not ready. However, as I was in Turin, I asked to see the Mirafiori factory and, at the end of my visit, I was given a superb little model of a FIAT 128 (I think, I am never sure about models).

Back home my son coveted this perfect little car and so I gave it to him: it became his favourite toy. But on one of my visits to his room, which was in a state of chaos, I promised him that if he did not put it in order, I would throw everything out of the window. On the following day the room was chaotic and I kept my promise. How could I do otherwise? Mothers must keep their word. But Owen was miserable: the one toy he really cared for had fallen four floors and was in pieces. So I suggested that he should write to Gianni Agnelli since he had stayed at his house and, after all, he was FIAT's chairman. Owen wrote. I didn't see the letter and some time went by.

A few weeks later a telephone call came from British FIAT and the manager was on the line. 'The car is ready,'

he said, 'but won't some spare parts do instead? At Brad-
ford we can make it as good as new.'

'No,' I said, 'it is really smashed up.'

'Which colour do you require?'

'Mine was blue, but it doesn't actually matter – any
colour will do,' said I.

Slightly embarrassed but very kindly he enquired how
it had fallen and from what height.

'Well, it was from the fourth floor, from my son's
bedroom window.'

There was another pause. 'But can you tell me how it
came to fall from there?'

Embarrassed, too, I had to confess that I myself had
thrown it out.

Visualizing the person with whom he was talking as a
mighty strong woman with the muscles of a Hercules, he
remained silent until, unfortunately, I added that it had
been my son's favourite toy.

A model of the car arrived on the following day.

David Niven

ACTOR

When I was a very impecunious young officer in the Regular Army aged nineteen (long before I became an actor and perhaps could have carried it off) I was invited to a Fancy Dress Ball at a *very* smart house in Leicestershire.

I took a lot of trouble and went as a clown complete with pompoms, a bladder, a string of evil-smelling sausages, and a very long false nose.

I arrived early, eager to meet the immensely smart and important people I knew would be there. Few cars were about when I showed up and the butler looked a little surprised, but anyway he opened the drawing-room door and announced me. Lots of smart and important people were indeed there and they were all in full evening dress.

I had got the right date but the wrong month.

The host and hostess insisted that I stay for dinner and I spent a miserable night in my greasepaint seated between two dowagers who never spoke to me and beneath the pitying eyes of butler and footman.

Sir Ralph Richardson

ACTOR

During the war I was given special leave from the Navy
to make a film about submarines. We were shooting in a
submarine lying in Liverpool Docks. On the way back to
our hotel after the day's activity, the late Charles Victor
and I shared a taxi to the Adelphi Hotel. Charles was
heavily made-up with full beard and dressed as a naval
officer. I was more or less playing myself and in civilian
clothes. We were just about to get into the lift at the
hotel when the manager approached me and expressed his
pleasure and gratification that I was patronizing his
august establishment.

'You will let me know,' he urged, 'if there's anything at
all we can do to make your stay comfortable.'

'A bottle of wine?' I suggested.

'We'll have it sent up to your room immediately.'

By this time Victor was growing a little impatient. He
was manifestly not to be included in the celebrations. The
manager accompanied us into the lift and pressed the
button for the sixth floor.

'If it's not too much trouble,' said Victor, 'I would like
to get out at the floor below.'

The manager reluctantly halted the lift and Charles got
out.

'Do you know, sir, who that was?' the manager said
to me, and before I could reply, he continued, 'That

was the actor Ralph Richardson.'

Who he imagined I was remains one of the great unsolved mysteries of the Second World War.

Glenda Jackson

ACTRESS

At about the age of fourteen I was sent to do the weekend shopping, taking my youngest sister aged three in her pram. I finished the shopping, returned home and only then discovered that pram plus baby had been left behind. I was not actually beaten until pram and baby had been safely returned.

Bricks in Literature

PROFESSOR JAMES SUTHERLAND

So far as the lexicographers are concerned, the first brick appears to have been dropped as recently as 1923, when someone wrote in *Punch*, 'I had dropped a brick, as you say.' The following year the phrase acquired unimpeachable respectability when John Galsworthy used it in *The White Monkey*. About twenty years later the irresistible modern desire for the emphatic ('My dear, it was absolutely *devastating*!') induced us to start dropping peculiarly heavy bricks, which were called 'clangers'. I take these facts from the recent *Supplement to the Oxford English Dictionary*, where 'to drop a brick' is defined as 'to commit a verbal indiscretion, make a "bloomer" '. The word 'bloomer', apparently a shortened form of 'a blooming error', has been traced back to Australian prison slang of about 1889, and has nothing to do with 'knickerbockers worn by women for bicycling'. But 'bloomer' was not (and so far as it remains current, is not) confined to verbal indiscretions. The same is true of 'making a gaffe', which we started saying in the first decade of the present century. We began 'putting a foot in it' a good deal earlier. In a slang dictionary of 1823 the phrase was glossed as 'to get into a scrape by speaking'; but it is older than that, going back to the last years of the eighteenth century, when a contributor wrote in the *Gentleman's Magazine* of 1798: 'The General has put his foot into it again.' We were already talking of a *faux pas* in the seventeenth century; but for some time the words usually meant 'an act which compromises one's reputation; a woman's lapse from virtue'.

That little burst of erudition is not meant to provoke astonishment that 'one small head could carry all he knew', but rather to suggest that our ancestors were just as likely to drop bricks as we are, though they didn't call them that. One of the most successful plays in the reign of Charles II was Dryden's *Sir Martin Mar-all*. Samuel Pepys thought it 'the best comedy ever was wrote', and went to see it ten times. 'I never laughed so in all my life,' he wrote in his diary after seeing it for the first time; 'I laughed till my head ached all the evening and night with the laughing.' What Pepys found so funny was Sir Martin's unfailing tendency to put his foot in it, to drop bricks both in speech and action, to goof every brilliant scheme he had thought up. Restoration comedy rested on a number of assumptions that are not always easy to define precisely, but one of them is awareness. The Restoration gentleman was socially alert, in entire control of himself and of the situation, and quick to respond and adapt himself to changing circumstances. Poor Sir Martin was at once 'dumb' and endlessly talkative, unaware but supremely confident, moving about, like Wordsworth's child, 'in worlds not realized'. (Sheridan's Mrs Malaprop, that inveterate dropper of verbal bricks, may be said to have moved among words not realized.)

Forty years after *Sir Martin Mar-all* and in the reign of Queen Anne, the dramatist whom her contemporaries called 'the celebrated Mrs Susanna Centlivre', had a resounding success with a similar play called *The Busy Body*. The luckless hero Marplot, 'a sort of silly fellow' who 'generally spoils all he undertakes, yet without design', goes from one blunder to another. On his first appearance his friend Charles, son of Sir Francis Gripe, introduces him to Sir George Airy, and Marplot promptly drops his first brick. The conversation gets round to Sir Francis, and Marplot cannot contain himself:

Marplot: 'Ah! he is a covetous, cheating, sanctified curmudgeon. That Sir Francis Gripe is a damn'd old—'
Charles: 'I suppose, friend, you forget that he is my father—'
Marplot: I ask your pardon, Charles; but it is for your sake I hate him.'

This is only the beginning; Marplot has still to boob and goof his way through five acts.

One doesn't have to be a fool to drop a brick, though it always helps. At all events, we sometimes come to grief because we are ignorant of some vital fact that we couldn't possibly have been expected to know. In his *Memoirs of Count de Grammont* Anthony Hamilton recounted one such blunder made by Richard Talbot, a gentleman of the bedchamber to the Duke of York, Charles II's brother. Writing long after the event, Hamilton got his dates wrong, and perhaps a good deal else; but the story he told could easily have happened. The Duke of York, who was every bit as promiscuous as his brother, had commenced an affair with Lady Carnegie, the wife of a Scottish peer. The lady was amenable, and everything was proceeding most satisfactorily, the more so as Lord Carnegie happened to be in Scotland paying his respects to his father, the Earl of Southesk. During this filial visit the old earl died, and his son duly returned to London, no longer Lord Carnegie, but Earl of Southesk. Rumours of what had been going on in his absence soon reached the new earl, but for the present he decided to do nothing more than keep a watch on his wife. The Duke for his part, realizing that he would now have to be rather more circumspect, made a point of never visiting the lady unless he was accompanied by a friend, who would give the occasion the necessary appearance of formality. I leave the rest to Anthony Hamilton:

> About this time Talbot returned from Portugal: this connection had taken place during his absence; and without knowing who Lady Southesk was, he had been informed that his master was in love with her.
>
> A few days after his arrival, he was carried, merely to keep up appearances, to her house by the Duke; and after being introduced, and some compliments having been paid on both sides, he thought it his duty to give his Royal Highness an opportunity to pay his compliments, and accordingly retired into the antechamber, which looked into the street, and placed himself at the window to view the people as they passed.
>
> He stood sentry, very attentive to his instructions, when he

saw a coach stop at the door, without being in the least concerned at it, and still less at a man whom he saw get out of it, and who he immediately heard coming upstairs.

The devil, who ought to be very civil upon such occasions, forgot himself in the present instance, and brought up Lord Southesk *in propria persona*. His Royal Highness's equipage had been sent home, because my lady had assured him that her husband was gone to see a bear and bull baiting, an entertainment in which he took great delight, and from whence he seldom returned until it was very late; so that Southesk, not seeing any equipage at the door, little imagined that he had such good company in his house.

But if he was surprised to see Talbot carelessly lolling in his wife's ante-chamber, his surprise was soon over. Talbot, who had not seen him since they were in Flanders, and never supposing that he had changed his name: 'Welcome, Carnegie, welcome, my good fellow,' said he, giving him his hand, 'where the devil have you been, that I have never been able to set eyes on you since we were at Brussels? What business brought you here? Do you likewise wish to see Lady Southesk? If that is your intention, my poor friend, you may go away again; for I must inform you the Duke of York is in love with her, and I will tell you in confidence that at this very time he is in her chamber.'

Southesk, confounded as one may suppose, had no time to answer all these fine questions. Talbot therefore attended him downstairs as his friend; and, as his humble servant, advised him to seek for a mistress elsewhere. Southesk, not knowing what else to do at that time, returned to his coach; and Talbot, overjoyed at the adventure, impatiently waited for the Duke's return, that he might acquaint him with it. But he was very much surprised to find that the story afforded no pleasure to those who had the principal share in it; and his greatest concern was that Carnegie had changed his name as if only to draw him into such a confidence.

99

It is not given to everyone to drop two such bricks in close succession. The Duke, however, must have forgiven Talbot, for on succeeding to the throne as James II he rewarded him (for rather more important services) with the title of Earl of Tyrconnel.

Dame Rebecca West

AUTHOR

Years ago in Washington a lift stopped and then shot up with only a nice looking lady and myself. We were both guests at a big dinner. I looked at her and said pathetically, 'Do tell me who you are.' And she said, 'Well, I am Mrs Truman, but I often wonder.'

I am bound to say that her smile was so sweet that I might have been giving her a bouquet rather than dropping a brick.

Bernard Levin

WRITER AND JOURNALIST

I claim (and there will be few challengers) to be the only
man who has ever introduced Lord Longford to his own
wife and, moreover, presented her under the name of
Lady Pamela Berry.

 What an extraordinarily short sentence for Bernard
Levin!

Prudence Leith

COOKERY AUTHOR AND RESTAURATEUR

I once had the marquee tent for someone's wedding party put up in the wrong garden – next door, in fact.

When I first started cooking for my living I had an Abyssinian cat who used to watch me filleting salmon and making gateaux from the window-sill. One day the telephone rang: 'Is that 229-0684?'

'Yes.'

'Is your name Benny?'

'No, but my cat's is.'

'Well what the hell is his name-tag doing in my salad?'

But my favourite catering disaster is the true story of the couple who went to the Far East on holiday. They wanted, besides their own supper, something to give their poodle. Pointing to the dog, they make international eating signs. The waiter understood, picked up the poodle and set off for the kitchen – only to return half-an-hour later with the roasted poodle on a platter.

Behram Kapadia

ART DIRECTOR

I was asked to take a photograph of Jimmy Greaves to appear on the jacket of his autobiography *This One's on Me* which tells the story of how pressures at the top drove him to alcoholism, wrecking his career and marriage. He was now painfully on the way to recovery with help from Alcoholics Anonymous.

I telephoned him with details of the photographic session and added, somewhat absently, 'If we finish early, Jimmy, how about a quick drink?'

Wendy Toye

DIRECTOR AND CHOREOGRAPHER

Deep in thought about a new production, I went to the ticket office in Leicester Square underground, asked for a ticket to Sloane Square, took from my handbag my powder compact, opened it and handed the man the powder-puff and – what's more – confidently waited for the change.

One night some years ago, suffering from the universal complaint, I was at Boots the chemist standing in a queue behind quite a number of people, with a lot more behind me, all waiting to get their drugs. When it came to my turn, I asked in my embarrassment for a large packet of Hemeroids. The chemist, thinking I was taking the mickey, kept saying wearily, 'Packet of what?' and I kept repeating louder each time, 'Hemeroids'. It wasn't until I heard the giggling queue behind me that I realized something was wrong – 'Germoloids' I should have been saying.

Lady Longford

BIOGRAPHER

I was married in November 1931 and was told by my kind and helpful mother-in-law that it was the correct thing to be presented at Court on marriage. So my name was put down for one of the early Courts the next year. Meanwhile I realized that I was going to have a baby in the following August. Should I cancel the Presentation?

'Oh, no, no one will notice. The first baby never shows.' Reassured, I practised my curtsey, but cautiously, not descending too low.

However, when the great day arrived, two things happened. The baby had evidently made a sudden spurt and, loaded with feathers and frills, I was unwieldy to say the least; and the graceful creature who was presented to their Majesties just before me, swept a magnificent curtsey right down to the ground. In the spirit of emulation, and forgetting what I had learnt at rehearsals, down I sank to the floor and – there remained for some of the worst seconds in my life. Could I rise again? I made several attempts to no effect. I could see the concerned courtiers on either side preparing to dash in and frog-march me away. At last, with a frantic heave I staggered to my feet and disappeared into the crowd, conscious that I had not only dropped a brick but might also have dropped a baby at the foot of the throne.

Barbara Kelly

TELEVISION PERSONALITY

I do rather tend to put my foot in it. Recently at an ambassadorial cocktail party, I became like a beleaguered 'dodgem' car, completely immobilized in the crush. Struggling to regain momentum and at least secure a canapé, I volunteered to no one in particular, 'This is just like the Black Hole of Calcutta'.

'Were you there?' enquired Mrs Indira Ghandi delightedly.

Michael Bartman

MARKETING DIRECTOR

It was a cold, rainy night and I was passing a friendly fish and chip shop when my wife and two children decided they would like to grab a bite to take home. The shop was in a busy road and I parked on the opposite side of the street and suggested they might like to stroll across in the rain and pick it up for themselves. However, as they all refused, I reluctantly negotiated the traffic and joined the queue and, some fifteen minutes later, found myself at the head of it, to receive four soggy bags of fish and chips. I dashed across the road, threw myself into the driving seat, flinging the greasy parcels at my wife beside me in the passenger seat and, muttering words of abuse, insisted that, in future, if the family wanted fish and chips they should bloody well go and fetch it themselves. My wife unaccountably started to scream, only it wasn't her but a total stranger! I looked up and through the windscreen to see my family in the identical car in front making strong come-hither movements.

'Where's the fish?' was their only comment when I rejoined them.

Norman St John-Stevas

MEMBER OF PARLIAMENT

I was going to Cambridge for the day and my car was being repaired. I said to my housekeeper, 'May I take your Mini?' She agreed and told me it was parked outside the door, but warned that it would not go very fast. I had some difficulty opening the door, but eventually got in and then had some difficulty getting the ignition key in, but it started up and off we went. Far from being slow, it positively flashed along.

I stopped on the motorway for petrol and found to my horror that there was a padlock on the petrol tank, but no key. So I asked the garage attendant for a jemmy and passed it off saying jokingly, 'If anyone saw this they might think I had stolen the car.'

'You'd be arrested,' he chuckled.

So off to Cambridge and back, and I had the car washed and filled with petrol as a thanks offering, and parked it outside the door.

Next day, when my housekeeper brought me my breakfast, she said, 'Why didn't you take my car yesterday?'

'I did,' said I.

'No,' she said, 'it's been outside the house all the time.'

'Nonsense,' I replied and jumping out of bed I went over to the window and, pointing, said, 'That is the one I took.'

'That's not mine. Mine's the one behind it.'

As the ghastly truth began to dawn I heard merry laughter outside and a voice say, 'Darling, your car's back.' I heard another voice say, 'Goodness, so it is, and look it's washed and full of petrol.'

I didn't wait to hear any more, but crawled back into bed and ate my boiled egg.

Years later I mentioned the story to my new secretary. 'Good heavens,' she screamed, 'that was my car.'

Dame Peggy Ashcroft

ACTRESS

I think my best piece of absent-mindness was during the war when we were playing *The Importance of Being Earnest* at the Phoenix, where it was excessively cold. After the matinée I put on my husband's largest pair of woollen socks. In the evening when the curtain went up on my first appearance as Cicely watering the roses in a pink muslin dress I looked down and saw that the socks were still on my feet. There was no chance of removing them – I could only bend at the knees and cover them up.

Nigel Nicolson

AUTHOR AND PUBLISHER

Early in 1940 I was a 2nd Lieutenant in the Grenadier Guards, stationed at Wellington Barracks, and was ordered to take forty men as reinforcements to the battalions in France. It was a simple job. I was to march them to Waterloo Station, entrain them for Dover, cross the Channel, deliver them to somewhere like Arras, and then return.

The war had scarcely started. There was no fighting in France, no bombing of London. But it was my first independent command, and I marched off my little detachment with inflated juvenile pride. We were accompanied by a small section of the regimental band, and one or two people cheered.

We crossed Westminster Bridge. On the far side I marked the entrance to Waterloo Station. 'Left wheel!' I cried. The columns responded. We passed under the great portal into the courtyard beyond which I expected to find the waiting train. There was no sign of it, nor of any locomotive activity whatever. Instead, tall office buildings enclosed us on all sides. A typist looked out of a window, then a dozen or more, tittering, and a few guardsmen risked a wave or two in response. The band faltered.

It was not Waterloo. It was the courtyard of the London County Council. The exit on the far side was barricaded, and there was no room for a u-turn. 'About turn!'

I commanded. While this manœuvre was possible, and indeed smartly executed, it left me and the band at the wrong end. We scurried round.

Then the second disaster occurred. I tripped on the kerb, fell into a puddle and rose drenched, filthy and diminished. Cries of derisive encouragement volleyed from the now crowded windows. My men were kinder. I signalled to the band that any musical accompaniment to a retreat would be inappropriate. We marched to Waterloo in total silence.

Magnus Magnusson

JOURNALIST AND BROADCASTER

When I was at Oxford, a fellow-undergraduate got himself engaged to a delightful undergraduette, a jewel of the county set in Wiltshire. She was the daughter of an Admiral; he was a totally unsuitable suitor (as he proved later by becoming a very successful journalist).

The betrothal was fiercely resisted by the girl's parents. But eventually they relented sufficiently to allow the young man to be invited for a country-house weekend. Everyone found it a difficult occasion, socially.

On the Saturday evening, Daddy had invited a lot of his seafaring cronies to dinner. Our hero found himself seated well below the salt, and not even next to his affianced.

The talk was all of seas and ships and sealing-wax, and our hero found himself out of his depth (he was reading P.P.E., which only qualified him to have opinions about cabbages and kings). So, for solace, he applied himself all too diligently to the claret.

Then, from the far end of the table where Daddy was holding court, there wafted down a word he felt he could recognize. The old sea-dogs were discussing 'buttocks', which, for the benefit of the uninitiated, means in nautical jargon 'the breadth of the ship astern from its tuck upwards'.

Here at last was a chance for our hero to make his mark on the conversation. Leaning forward, he bellowed up the table: '*Buttocks!* Did you say *buttocks?* My future wife has a splendid pair!'

The marriage did not take place.

 It's obviously Magnus's own experience, so we've taken
the liberty of including him in the illustration.

Graham Payn

ACTOR

I was only seventeen. I was playing a very small part in *The Tempest* on television at Alexandra Palace before the Second World War, while Peggy Ashcroft had the enormous responsibility of playing Miranda. We met in the corridor at the awful moment just before the performance (performances went out 'live' in those days) and Miss Ashcroft very sweetly wished me good luck.

'Thank you,' I replied, 'I am so nervous.'

'Don't worry, so am I.'

'Well,' I said, 'you have every reason to be.'

Dannie Abse

DOCTOR AND POET

That particular Friday, because I was going to spend the weekend in South Wales, I hoped to leave work early but the relief radiographer proved to be incompetent and slow. All the x-rays sent to me were either under-developed or overdeveloped, under-penetrated or over-penetrated, or partially fogged. Patient after patient had to be returned to the x-ray department for a repeat x-ray.

At last it seemed that there were no more x-rays for me to read and it was time to leave. I would catch a later train from Paddington than I had intended. I was at the door when the telephone on my desk again rang insistently; it was the inept radiographer.

'Could you hang on, sir?' he said. 'There's one more patient. Dr Wicks would like you to report on it now. When it's ready, I'll bring the x-ray to you.'

I can't remember exactly how I responded; I suppose I gracelessly said something like, 'All right, but don't bugger up the film this time.' I returned to my desk and to pass the time read the current *British Medical Journal*. Then I looked at my watch. I had missed another train and now half an hour had passed since the radiographer called me.

I was half-way through a paper on '*Pseudomyxoma Peritonei*: An Unusual Case' when I decided that enough was enough and I stamped out of the room towards the x-ray department, where I at once encountered the radiographer emerging from the dark room. 'It's just developed, doctor,' he said before I could say a word. 'Will you read it wet?'

In the dark room there is a screen on which wet x-ray films can be hung. The radiographer placed the film on it and turned a switch so that the screen lit up brilliantly behind the x-ray. I looked at it astonished. The posterior-anterior view of the patient's chest – the usual view – was at an extraordinary tilted angle of forty-five degrees: the left shoulder was way up, the right shoulder way down. I had never seen anything like it.

Sarcastically I tilted my head at an angle of forty-five degrees as I scrutinized it and said tightly, 'How the hell did you manage that?'

'Well ...' he said.

'For God's sake,' I roared, 'all day you've messed things up and now this is utterly skew-whiff.'

'The patient's behind you, sir,' the radiographer urgently interrupted me.

I turned from him towards the open dark room door, put on a suitable smile and approached the patient in order to reassure him.

'Your x-ray is normal,' I said. 'It's fine, though it's tilted somewhat. The radiographer has somehow cleverly contrived to make you look like a cripple. That's what I was complaining to him about. Don't *you* worry.'

'Can I go now?' asked the patient.

'Of course,' I said smiling benignly.

And the patient, unsmiling, rose, one-legged, to limp pronouncedly over the brown linoleum of the x-ray department and through the door to disappear from my sight but never entirely from my mind. I turned to the radiographer who lounged, rather than stood, against the wall, his face a study of sweet magnificent triumph.

Heather Sherratt

BOOK DESIGNER

I was sitting on a crowded bus about a year after I got married when a young man leapt on, came and stood opposite me, and said, 'Hello,' looking obviously delighted to see me.

I gazed blankly at the beaming face, puzzled, until I finally asked, 'Who are you?'

'I'm your husband,' came the injured reply.

André Previn

COMPOSER AND CONDUCTOR

The process of adopting a Vietnamese orphan is, quite correctly, fraught with difficulties. My family has now been graced by these children three times, but I still remember one slightly insane moment during the first adoption attempt. Visiting my house, prior to the final sanction, was a remarkable lady named Rosemary Taylor, who had led a selfless existence in Saigon, running an orphanage. I doubt whether I will ever meet anyone more suited to eventual sainthood than this extraordinary woman. She was a weekend guest in my house in Surrey and, needless to say, we underestimated her sense of humour and her sense of occasion, and bent over backwards to make everything with which she came into contact seem to spring from the pages of an ideal home magazine.

Now, at the time, my small sons were addicted to an admixture of health-food cereals, which they consumed with gusto each morning. I personally thought it vile, but they loved it, and I presume it was good for them. The stuff was kept in one of several large glass containers in the kitchen. On her first morning in my house, Miss Taylor appeared for breakfast. She asked for cereal, and I gave her a large bowlful, lauding the energy-giving qualities of this blameless concoction. She poured milk over it, disdained the use of sugar, and fell to. She ate in silent contemplation,

and if there was any dissatisfaction on her face, I missed it. Finally, the bowl empty, she pushed it away. 'I have to be honest with you,' she said, 'I'm not really crazy about it.' My eyes happened to glance at the various glass jars around the cupboard. A realization hit me. I blanched. Finally I managed an answer: 'Actually I'm not surprised,' I said as gently as possible, 'I've just made you eat a large dish of hamster food.'

Michael Noakes

ARTIST

I had been commissioned to paint a portrait of the newly-appointed Chief of Defence Staff. Since there was to be a domestic background in the picture, the first two sittings were to be held in his home rather than in my studio.

I arrived and laid out my equipment happily, and we tried out his chair in various positions in different lights. My first error was when, trying to be helpful, I attempted to pass his Field Marshal's baton to him (delicate gold filigree top, velvet-covered, presented to him by the Queen just two weeks before). Somehow I missed – and it dropped with an echoing thwang into a tin waste-paper bin. That, not surprisingly, did not go down very well.

Determined to prove that painters are not really clumsy idiots, I set to work – deliberately painting with deft, rhythmic arm movements. But I knew, as that fully-loaded brush sprang out of my hand and hurtled like a rocket across his drawing-room, that it was going to touch down on the one bit of the Aubusson carpet, in the far corner, that I had not protected with dust-sheets ... and Alazarin Crimson, just right for painting the ribbon of the Order of the Bath, is unfortunately so powerful a colour that it is virtually impossible to remove the stain completely.

We had to stop for twenty minutes whilst I did what I could to put right the damage with my turpentine and his

detergent. Before starting again, I asked if I might wash my hands. The Field Marshal was obviously only too glad to be rid of me for a bit, and directed me to the little cloakroom by the front door.

While there, I thought I would take the opportunity first to spend a penny; as I washed my hands, though, I became aware that the loo was making the strangest noises. I went across to have a look at it and, incapable of action, I watched as the water-level gurgled over the brim and several gallons were deposited all over the floor.

The next time I had a sitting at the Field Marshal's home, I was filled with good resolutions as I drove up to the front door. He, looking slightly strained I thought, greeted me there. He was, though, still surprisingly courteous: holding the door wide open for me as I carried my portable easel through, he gave me a weak smile. 'Good morning, Field Marshal!' I beamed, as I eased past him with a caricature of extreme care. Then the collapsible leg on the easel fell open, and removed a large chunk of the door.

Michael Aspel

BROADCASTER

I was once, and only once, invited to a reception at the Iranian Embassy. A well-meaning colleague at the BBC provided me with what he described as an all-purpose greeting in Farsi, which I learned by heart. When I was introduced to the Ambassador, a large hairy man, I recited the phrase perfectly. He gave me a wintry smile and moved away. An interpreter explained that I had just told the Ambassador that I would not exchange the moles on his cheeks for all the riches in Samarkand and Bokhara. No wonder the poor fellow looked puzzled: His Excellency was wondering, no doubt, who had told me about them.

Magnus Pyke

SCIENTIST AND TELEVISION
PERSONALITY

It is well known – or by now it should be, since Gaspard
Coriolis wrote a paper about it in 1835 – that in the
Northern Hemisphere bath water corkscrews its way
down the plug-hole in an anti-clockwise direction. You
need to understand this if you are concerned with the
exact placement of communications satellites up in the
sky. There I was, with a full-scale transparent bath, explaining the reason for this to the multitudinous television
audience, telephoning Sydney to allow a scientific colleague there to describe how differently bath water be-
haves in Australia, sending a man to Nanuki in Kenya
where bath water runs away left-handed or right-handed
with equal facility, plug-holes being exactly on the Equa-
tor there. And then, when I pulled the plug out in Leeds,
the water started twisting round (or so the little floating
flag seemed to show) the wrong way.

And yet ... and yet.... Goaded from my humiliation
by a gesticulating cameraman, I turned back to look at the
bath water again. I found that it *was* twisting anti-clockwise after all. If you imagine the long limp sausage of
water extending up from the plug to the surface, when the
bottom starts twisting left-handed, the top drifts round
for a while right-handed – which is what had caused my
heart to sink – before the whole thing gradually gets itself
together and (in the Northern Hemisphere) spins round its

anti-clockwise way. My brick did indeed start to drop, but Gaspard, dead though he may have been for nearly a hundred and fifty years, caught it nicely for me.

 Unbelievable, isn't it?

William Douglas-Home

PLAYWRIGHT

In early youth, while sitting with the grown-ups at lunch, I remember hearing my elderly Aunt Margaret assuring a retired schoolmaster, who had asked her if the county she lived in in Wales were over-populated, that it was, in fact, 'very sparsely copulated indeed'.

Warren Mitchell

ACTOR

Scene: Sir Peter Hall's office at the National Theatre,
Thames flowing outside, the hock inside, just finished the
smoked salmon, my reward for being terribly talented in
Death of a Salesman.
Sir Peter: You know I'd like to see you tackle *The*
           Tempest.
Me: Caliban?

Sir Peter: No, Prospero.

Me: You're joking.

Sir Peter: No, you see the part is often misunderstood. Prospero is concerned with power – it's a great play.

Me: I'm not mad about it. Saw it once at the Old Vic with Sir John. Mind you, it was an awful production, I couldn't believe it. Do you know what the director did?

Slow freeze. Cut to M.C.U. Sir Peter – tiny smile playing round his lips, he nods.

Sir Peter: Yes, it was my production.

Me: Can I have another glass of hock, please?

 Of course everyone knows that M.C.U. is maximum close up.

Diana Rigg

ACTRESS

.

I was in my dressing-room at the Old Vic changing after a performance of *Jumpers* and chatting to my mother when there was a knock at the door. The visitor turned out to be Albert Finney, who was rehearsing *Hamlet*, the next production in the theatre. My mother, anxious to prove herself in the theatrical swim, turned to Albert Finney, enquiring brightly, 'And when are you going to give us your Hammy?'

Theo Cowan

PUBLICIST

One day, as I rushed out of my office late for lunch, I found a taxi waiting at the kerb, opened the door and jumped in, shouting my destination to the driver. A moment later I realized I was sitting on the lap of another passenger. As I am of rather unusually heavy build, my first thought was that I might have done him an injury. I manœuvred myself into the space beside him and enquired, 'Are you all right, sir?' Obviously temporarily winded, he seemed unable to speak. At this moment the cabbie turned round and said, 'I already have a fare,' whereupon I burst into uncontrollable laughter. I scrambled out crab-like and, regaining the pavement, watched a little man in a blue suit sitting bolt upright and staring fixedly ahead, being driven slowly away. The last thing he expected, presumably, when he hailed the cab was that he would be engaged so soon in a game of musical chairs.

William Whitelaw

MEMBER OF PARLIAMENT

I was attending a reception at the American Embassy several years ago and was introduced to an American whom I did not know. After I had spoken to him for some time, I went to a friend and said, 'Do tell me, who is that American I was talking to about golf? He doesn't appear to have much sense of humour.' My friend replied: 'Bob Hope.'

Life with Danny, Emma, Christopher and Jane

As this book has been compiled to aid the National Society for Autistic Children, it might be helpful to describe briefly what autism is and to give some idea of what life is like for some children and their families.

Autism is a syndrome present from birth or beginning almost invariably in the first thirty months of life. Responses to auditory and visual stimuli are abnormal and there are usually severe difficulties in the understanding of spoken language. Speech is delayed in developing; if it does develop, it is characterized by echolalia, the reversal of pronouns, immature grammatical structure, and inability to use abstract terms. There is generally an impairment in the social use of both verbal and gestural language. Problems in social relationships are most severe before the age of five and include an impairment in the development of eye-to-eye gaze, social attachments, and co-operative play. Ritualistic behaviour is usual and may include abnormal routines, resistance to change, attachment to odd objects, and stereotyped patterns of play. The capacity for abstract or symbolic thought and for imaginative play is diminished. Intelligence ranges from severely subnormal to normal or above. Performance is usually better on tasks involving rote memory of visuospatial skills than on those requiring symbolic or linguistic skills.

The following anecdotes, which first appeared in 'Communication', the magazine of the National Society for Autistic Children, were collected by the children's parents over several years.

To know autistic children is to love them; but to love them it is necessary to develop a very thick skin. They are outspoken and direct to the point of insult by normal standards. They can be agile and hyperactive to the point of damage and danger, and then siblings can suffer physically and mentally from their obsessions and rituals. In spite of all this, the awkward situations that occur are often quite funny when you remember them later.

Danny was at his first concert. To keep him from fidgeting, we handed him a pair of opera glasses. At first this was a blessed diversion, but for some reason, every time the horns sounded, he would turn round in his seat and carefully adjust the focus on to a woman sitting just behind us.

At first the woman ignored this scrutiny, but as the horn-playing became more frequent I noted her face changing – from a one-time pink, it appeared to take on an ominous shade of puce.

In the end I turned round and whispered an apology. 'He's handicapped,' I added.

Puce-face glared. 'You might have told me before,' she spat.

Incensed, I retorted, 'What do you expect me to do? Stick a notice on his back saying "I am handicapped"?'

'It would help,' she answered.

The incident could well have closed at this juncture, had it not been for Deborah – always a champion of her brother – who rounded on Puce-face. 'In that case,' she said, 'you ought to have a notice on your front saying "I am cross".'

★

Danny was belatedly going through a phase of imaginative play – goblins, fairies, giants, little people. The house was full of them. Elaine's cello teacher – a charming and shy man – arrived at our home for his first visit. Danny, a normal-looking eleven-year-old, approached him. 'Hey,' he said in a confidential tone, 'I think you're really a fairy.'

★

Emma had a particularly nasty habit of sinking her teeth into her brothers and sister when frustrated. There were days when a ring at the front door conjured up visions of some benevolent N.S.P.C.C. inspector shaking his head in utter disbelief that a two-year-old's arm, bruised from wrist to shoulder could be caused by autistic teeth. We watched her, of course, as best we could and pounced to remove the two-year-old when sister bared her teeth. It was the seven-year-old who suffered the final indignity. Having been warned not to put her hands through the bars of the cot where her autistic sister was warming up for her all-night trampoline session, there was a wail of anguish. No sympathy from a weary mother: 'I told you not to put your hand near her.' The response was heart-rending: 'I didn't, it was my nose – I only wanted to kiss her good-night.'

★

At the age of eight, Christopher decided that a friendly approach might be 'a good thing'. On entering the Primary School where he attended a special class, he bounced up to the Headmaster and said, 'Morning Usherwood, d'you want a kiss?'

At the age of ten, Christopher greeted guests with the invaluable information, 'You mustn't pee down the drain!'

★

Most people reading this book may feel they have never actually met an autistic child, but think carefully – maybe you are fortunate enough to be able to say you remember one. Perhaps you are one of the people our family used to meet when we took our autistic daughter out.

Maybe you can remember lying peacefully on the beach when, for some unknown reason, a very attractive toddler suddenly jumped to her feet and ran down the beach; nothing unusual so far – but – perhaps did feel something was different about her, for instead of running on the sand (as normal, boring people do) Jane thudded over you. Now, it may be that you are fond of children, but one foot in your face and one in the middle of your stomach cannot, I am sure, be the best way to further relationships between children and adults. I am sorry we did not stop to apologize, but look at it from our point of view: wasn't it better to catch her? And anyway,

143

as you were doubled up gasping for breath, it hardly seemed fair to disturb you again.

If you still don't remember us, maybe it was your sausage Jane stole as we were sitting down in the restaurant. One minute you had egg, sausage and chips; the next you just had egg and chips. But you must be honest – you never really saw it go. You just felt the little girl two tables away munching a sausage had something to do with it, but you couldn't be *sure*, could you?

Perhaps you met Jane and me out shopping. When Jane wanted some sweets and I very firmly said no, a favourite trick of hers was to take off her pants and hurl them in the air.

So please think back – maybe we have met before. Thank you for buying this book and you never know, you could be the next lucky person to meet us.